DAVID'S SECRET

THE LOST PATH TO A WHOLE AND HEALTHY SOUL

TOM CORNELL

ABOUT THE AUTHOR

Tom Cornell is the Senior Leader of SOZO Church in Washington state, founder of Walk in the Light International and SOZO Network. Tom is married to his beautiful wife Katy and lives in the Puget Sound area with her and their three kids. He has been in ministry pastoring and teaching the body of Christ since 2008.

He has a passion to see the body of Christ moving from people with an orphan mindset to that of sonship; equipping the body to do the work of Jesus resulting in seeing the Kingdom of God manifested here on earth.

DAVID'S SECRET

The Lost Path to a Whole and Healthy Soul

TOM CORNELL

SOZO PUBLISHING

Contents

Introduction

THE SOUL WAS NEVER MEANT TO BE SILENT

There was a time in my life when I had already experienced deliverance. I had been healed in powerful ways. I had seen the power of the Holy Spirit cast out darkness, break generational strongholds, and restore shattered identity. But even after all of that—there were moments when I would feel a pressure in my chest. A tightness I couldn't explain. A heaviness that prayer didn't lift and worship didn't immediately dissolve. It didn't feel like sin. It wasn't the enemy attacking. But it was there. And it wouldn't go away.

What I came to realize is this: healing and deliverance are powerful, but not complete if you never learn to deal with what your soul is carrying. The truth is, my soul was still trying to speak. But I had not yet learned how to listen.

This book is about that journey—my own, and the one I've walked with countless others. A journey into the often-neglected world of the soul. Not just the realm of thoughts to be corrected, but emotions to be released, pain to be processed, and needs to be recognized and met in the presence of God.

We Take Thoughts Captive — But Emotions Must Be Released

Scripture tells us in 2 Corinthians 10:5 to take every thought captive to the obedience of Christ. And that's critical. We have to deal with the thoughts, lies, and belief systems that exalt themselves above the truth of God. But what many of us do instead is take our emotions captive. We stuff them down, silence them, pretend they don't exist —and we call it maturity.

The result? People who know how to rebuke demons but don't know how to grieve. People who can quote Scripture but don't know how to identify or express what they feel. And eventually, they break under the weight of unprocessed pain. And I was one of them.

When the Soul Suffocates, the Flesh Compensates

When we don't deal with the emotional weight our soul carries, we end up developing coping mechanisms instead of pursuing healing. This is one of the roots behind addictions that plague so many believers—pornography, alcohol, drug use, binge eating, emotional withdrawal, even excessive ministry. We don't know how to feel, so we run. We don't know how to sit with the ache, so we escape it.

What I've learned is this: your soul has needs. Not carnal cravings—God designed needs. The need for connection. The need for comfort. The need to feel safe.

The need to be heard. The need to process pain in a healthy, godly way. And when those needs aren't met in truth and love, the soul begins to break down. And the body—and behavior—often follows.

The Silent Crisis — Especially for Men

Though this journey applies to all of us, I've seen it especially among men. Many were raised by fathers or grandfathers who had little emotional vocabulary. Maybe they were taught—directly or indirectly—that feelings are weakness, tears are shameful, and emotions are for women. So they hardened. And they've been bleeding internally ever since.

This book isn't a call to be soft—it's a call to be whole. It's not about glorifying emotion—it's about honoring how God made us. Because until we learn to guard our heart without hardening it... until we learn to listen to the cries of our soul and respond with compassion... we'll keep raising up believers who are strong in public but broken in private. And the enemy loves to attack in that gap.

A Kingdom Approach to Soul Wholeness

This book is not about psychology alone. It's about the Kingdom of God invading the soul. It's about discovering that deliverance is the beginning, not the end. That you can be saved and still need healing. That taking your thoughts captive is essential—but it must be paired with learning how to release your emotions and meet your soul's needs in God's presence.

Jesus is the Shepherd of your soul—not just your spirit.

He doesn't just save you for Heaven—He walks with you in your humanity. He knows how to restore the fragments of your heart, untangle the knots of confusion, and remove the bitter roots that have been rotting beneath the surface for years.

What This Book Will Teach You

In the pages ahead, we'll explore how to:

- Identify the difference between unhealthy thoughts and unprocessed emotions
- Understand how suppressed emotions affect your mind, body, and spirit
- Learn from David's example in the Psalms— honest, messy, raw, and redemptive
- Heal the deeper pain that doesn't just go away with a verse or a shout
- Break free from coping patterns by learning to name and meet your soul's needs
- Cultivate a daily rhythm of soul care, healing, and emotional wholeness
- Create a safe culture where others can be healed, not just helped

This is not just a book for your mind—it's an invitation to your heart. An invitation to stop stuffing, stop running, and stop faking peace. It's time to listen to your soul again. To bring it into the presence of Jesus. And to let Him do what only He can—make you whole from the inside out.

Let's begin.

ONE

The Soul God Created

UNDERSTANDING THE MIND, WILL, AND EMOTIONS

We were created in the image of God—spirit, soul, and body. Most believers know they have a body and a spirit, but very few understand what it means to have a soul, let alone how to care for it. And yet the soul is where so much of our daily life is lived. It's the seat of our thoughts, our emotions, and our will. It is where our memories live, where our identity is formed, and where our inner responses to pain and truth are shaped.

When your soul is healthy, life flows. When it's neglected, suppressed, or fragmented—everything starts to feel off. You might still pray, lead, serve, and even cast out demons. But beneath the surface, something feels disconnected. And that disconnect is where the enemy likes to work.

What Is the Soul?

The soul is the part of you that thinks, feels, and chooses. In Scripture, the Greek word often used is psyche

—from which we get the word psychology. The Hebrew word *nephesh* speaks of breath or life—the inner essence of a person. It's not your physical body, and it's not your born-again spirit. It's the inner terrain of your humanity.

We see the parts of the soul reflected in verses like:

- Mind — "Set your minds on things above…" (Col. 3:2 NIV)
- Will — "Not my will but Yours be done." (Luke 22:42 NIV)
- Emotions — "Jesus wept." (John 11:35 NIV) and "He was moved with compassion." (Matt. 9:36 NIV)

The soul was designed to partner with the spirit and lead the body. But after the Fall, man's soul often took the lead—and became shaped by trauma, fear, and sin. And even after salvation, many believers still live from a wounded or un-renewed soul, because they've never learned to bring that part of themselves to Jesus for healing.

The Soul Speaks—If We're Willing to Listen

Your soul is not just a passive container—it's a communicator. It has a voice. It sends signals when something's wrong. But what many of us were taught, especially men, is to silence those signals. We were told, directly or indirectly, "Don't cry. Don't feel. Don't talk about that. Just be strong." And so we learned to stuff it.

But suppressed emotions don't disappear. They sit in the basement of the soul, collecting pressure. Eventually, they leak out in other ways—anger, isolation, addiction, anxiety, or sickness. It's like a warning light on a car dashboard. If you ignore it long enough, the engine starts to fail.

That's why one of the most important truths you can embrace is this: emotions are not your enemy. They are messengers. And when you bring them to Jesus, they become doors to healing.

We Take Thoughts Captive — We Don't Take Emotions Hostage

Many believers know how to deal with thoughts—but not with feelings. We learn to rebuke lies, renew the mind, quote Scripture, and tear down strongholds—and all of that is essential. But somewhere along the way, we confuse the process.

Instead of taking thoughts captive, we start trying to take our emotions captive. We suppress them, spiritualize them, or shame ourselves for even having them. But here's the truth: *you can't rebuke a feeling. You can only release it.*

You can't cast out sadness. You can't bind and loose grief. You can't overcome trauma by ignoring it. What you can do is take those emotions to the One who created your soul in the first place.

David is the blueprint for this. He wept, lamented, questioned, grieved—and still was called "a man after God's own heart." Why? Because he didn't hide what he felt. He brought it into God's presence. He poured it out like a drink offering.

"Pour out your heart before Him; God is a refuge for us." (Psalm 62:8 NKJV)

When the Soul Is Ignored, the Body Pays the Price

Modern science and ancient Scripture agree: when the soul is unhealthy, the body suffers.

- Proverbs 14:30 NIV says, "A heart at peace gives life to the body, but envy rots the bones."
- Psalm 32:3–4 NIV describes David's unconfessed pain like this: "When I kept silent, my bones wasted away… My strength was sapped as in the heat of summer."

When we don't process grief, disappointment, or fear, our bodies often take the hit. We start to carry stress in our muscles. Our sleep gets disrupted. Our immune system weakens. Anxiety builds. And over time, we become fatigued, reactive, or physically sick—and we don't know why.

We pray for healing, and rightly so. But sometimes, what we need is not just physical healing—it's soul healing. God doesn't just want to remove symptoms. He wants to restore the source.

The Needs of the Soul Are Real—and Often Misunderstood

Every soul has needs: the need to feel safe. The need to be loved. The need to be seen. The need to process pain. The need to rest. The need for connection. The need to be comforted. These are not weaknesses—they are design features. When those needs go unmet or get violated, pain enters the soul. And that pain will speak—either directly or indirectly.

This is why so many fall into sin, not from rebellion but from misdirected need.

- Porn becomes a counterfeit for connection.
- Alcohol becomes a substitute for peace.
- Isolation feels safer than risking vulnerability.
- Numbness feels easier than facing what's inside.

These are not just bad habits. They are warning signs. They are survival mechanisms. And they are invitations— if we're willing to listen.

The Spirit of God Ministers to the Soul

Jesus said in Luke 4:18 NKJV, "He has sent Me to heal the brokenhearted…"

This isn't just a poetic phrase—it's a mission statement. Jesus came not only to save your spirit but to restore your soul.

The same Spirit who gives you power to preach the gospel also wants to sit with you in your weeping. He wants to walk with you into the memory that still hurts. He wants to uncover the roots that formed when you were 5, 15, or 35. He wants to renew the patterns in your mind and the beliefs in your heart.

And He's not afraid of your mess. He already knows what's there.

Your Soul is Safe With Jesus

Maybe you've never learned how to sit with your soul. Maybe you were never given permission to feel what you feel. Maybe you've confused spiritual strength with emotional silence. But Jesus is inviting you into something better. Not emotional chaos. Not soul-centered living. But wholeness—where your thoughts are renewed by truth, your emotions are healed by love, and your decisions flow from peace, not pain.

He's not asking you to perform. He's asking you to be honest. He's not calling you to be perfect—He's calling you to be present. To stop running. To stop hiding. And to let Him in.

Reflection Questions

1. What was I taught growing up about emotions—especially as a man or woman?

2. Do I regularly notice and name what I feel, or do I tend to stuff it down?

3. What are some behaviors in my life that might be coping mechanisms rather than freedom?

4. What does it look like to bring my emotions into the presence of God this week?

TWO

Taking Every Thought Captive

BREAKING AGREEMENT WITH MENTAL
STRONGHOLDS

M ost spiritual warfare begins with a whisper in the
mind. It rarely starts with full-blown deception or
obvious sin. It begins with a thought —just one—that
contradicts the truth of God. A seed of fear. A subtle accu-
sation. A shame-based conclusion. A quiet suggestion that
something is wrong with you or that God isn't who He says
He is.

This is why Scripture commands us in 2 Corinthians
10:5 NKJV to "take every thought captive to the obedience of Christ." Because thoughts are not just fleeting
ideas. Thoughts are agreements—they are spiritual door-
ways. And if you leave them unchallenged, those thoughts
will shape your emotions, your choices, and eventually your
life.

Thoughts Are More Powerful Than We Think

Every thought you entertain is either rooted in truth or
deception. It either partners with the Holy Spirit or the

voice of the accuser. Thoughts become beliefs, beliefs become behaviors, and behaviors become habits. So if the enemy can control your thinking, he can control your direction.

That's why the battlefield of the mind is so central in spiritual life. Deliverance is real. Demons are real. But many believers are not being tormented by a demon— they're being tormented by a lie they've believed for too long.

- "I'll never be enough."
- "I can't trust anyone."
- "God must be disappointed in me."
- "I have to perform to be accepted."
- "I'm just wired this way—I'll never change."
  None of these are just thoughts—they're strongholds.

What Is a Stronghold?

In biblical terms, a stronghold is a fortified place. In the natural, it's a structure that provides safety, stability, and protection. But spiritually, a stronghold can either be a defense of truth or a fortress of lies.

2 Corinthians 10:4–5 NKJV says:

"The weapons of our warfare are not carnal but mighty in God for pulling down strongholds, casting down arguments and every high thing that exalts itself against the knowledge of God..."

A stronghold is any mindset that is resistant to God's truth. It's a mental fortress built brick by brick with thoughts that oppose God's nature, Word, and character. The longer that thought is left unchallenged, the stronger the stronghold becomes.

How Strongholds Are Built in the Soul

1. Pain happens (trauma, loss, rejection, abandonment).
2. Interpretation follows ("It's my fault," "I can't trust," "God let me down").
3. Agreement forms ("This is just the way it is").
4. Repetition reinforces the lie until it becomes a lens.

And then that lens begins to filter everything:

- You don't see people clearly—you project your pain.
- You don't see God clearly—you project disappointment.
- You don't see yourself clearly—you walk in shame and insecurity.

This is why taking thoughts captive isn't just about positive thinking. It's about spiritual warfare. It's about breaking false agreements and replacing them with truth that sets you free.

Recognizing the Voice of the Lie

Lies rarely shout. They often sound like your own voice. They blend in with your internal dialogue. They feel familiar—almost comfortable. But here are a few ways to recognize them:

- They produce shame instead of conviction.
- They create fear and control rather than trust and peace.
- They lead you to hide, perform, or self-punish.
- They distort God's heart—making Him seem distant, angry, or indifferent.
- They leave you feeling stuck, powerless, or disqualified.

The good news is: you don't have to believe every thought that enters your mind. You have the authority in Christ to test, challenge, and replace it.

The Process of Taking Thoughts Captive

1. Identify the Thought

Slow down enough to notice what's running through your mind. Especially in moments of pressure, conflict, or temptation—what are you believing in that moment?

2. Compare it with God's Truth

Does this thought align with Scripture and the character of Jesus? Or does it oppose God's promises?

3. Break Agreement

Say it out loud: "I break agreement with the lie that _____." Call it what it is.

4. Replace it with the Truth

Declare the truth of God's Word: "I come into agreement with the truth that _____."

5. Repeat until Rewired

This is not always one-and-done. Many lies are layered or reinforced over years. But as you consistently renew your mind, your brain literally rewires and your soul realigns.

Jesus Confronted Thoughts with Truth

In the wilderness, Jesus didn't ignore the enemy's suggestions—He responded to each with, "It is written." He modeled how to fight lies with truth—not emotion, not argument, not performance. You don't defeat lies by being strong. You defeat lies by standing in truth.

When Captive Thoughts Affect Emotions

Here's where this ties to emotional healing: every time you believe a lie, it will produce a corresponding emotion.

- Believing "God has forgotten me" will lead to despair.
- Believing "People always leave" will lead to fear and isolation.
- Believing "I'm not good enough" will lead to shame or striving.
- Believing "Nothing ever changes" will lead to hopelessness.

This is why some people are not emotionally free—not because their feelings are wrong, but because their beliefs are toxic. And no amount of prayer will fix a lie you continue to believe. You don't just need emotional release —you need mental renewal. And when those two come together, the soul begins to heal.

A Kingdom Mind Is a Captive Mind

To walk in Kingdom peace, you have to submit your inner world to Kingdom truth. That means not just being aware of what you're thinking—but being willing to surrender it. A captive mind is not a passive mind—it's one brought under the rulership of Jesus.

- A Kingdom mind says, "My thoughts don't rule me—truth does."
- A Kingdom mind says, "If it's not in Heaven, I don't have to think it here."
- A Kingdom mind says, "Jesus gets the final word over what I believe."

This is the beginning of inner freedom.

Reflection Questions

1. What recurring thoughts or beliefs do I hear in my inner dialogue?

2. Have I made agreements with any lies about myself, God, or others?

3. What emotions in my life could be traced back to toxic thinking?

4. Am I willing to break those agreements and begin replacing them with truth?

THREE

When We Try to Silence Emotions

THE DANGER OF EMOTIONAL SUPPRESSION

You can cast out demons. You can memorize Scripture. You can rebuke every lie and still find yourself stuck. Why? Because truth alone doesn't always address pain. You can know truth in your head and still carry grief, disappointment, fear, or shame in your heart.

This is where many believers get frustrated. They've taken every thought captive. They've gone through deliverance. They've fasted, worshiped, and rebuked every spirit they can name. And yet... something still feels heavy inside. Something's still lodged deep in the soul. The issue is not what they believe—it's what they've never allowed themselves to feel.

The Soul Can't Heal When the Emotions Are Silenced

For many of us, somewhere along the way, we were taught that emotions are dangerous. We were told that if we want to be spiritually strong, we have to stuff down what we feel and just "walk by faith." So instead of learning how to process emotion, we learned how to hide it. Suppress it. Spiritualize it. Or worse—shame it.

But here's the truth: your emotions are not the problem. Unprocessed emotion is. Think of your emotions like the nervous system of your soul. Pain tells you where the injury is. Anger tells you something unjust happened. Fear warns that something feels unsafe. Sadness tells you something was lost.

If you never learn to listen, you'll never know what your soul actually needs. And a soul whose emotions are shut down is like a body full of painkillers—numb, unaware, and vulnerable to deeper damage.

Suppression vs. Surrender

There's a difference between not letting emotions lead and not letting emotions speak. Jesus didn't let His emotions lead Him, but He didn't deny them either.

- He wept at Lazarus' tomb.
- He groaned in anguish in Gethsemane.
- He was moved with compassion when He saw the broken.
- He expressed frustration with religious hypocrisy.
- He rejoiced with His disciples.

Jesus was fully emotional and fully sinless. Which means having emotion isn't weakness—it's human. It's godly. It's part of the imago Dei—the image of God in you. Suppression says, "Shut up." Surrender says, "Speak, and I'll bring it to Jesus."

The Cost of Silenced Emotion

Suppressed emotions don't just go away—they settle. And when they settle, they begin to shape everything: your tone of voice, your ability to trust, your stress level, your spiritual sensitivity. Some of the anxiety people are fighting isn't from demons or dysfunction—it's the sound of a soul trying to be heard.

Proverbs 14:30 ESV says, *"A tranquil heart gives life to the flesh, but envy makes the bones rot."*

David said in Psalm 32:3–4 NIV, *"When I kept silent, my bones wasted away... my strength was sapped."*

This is more than poetic language. There is scientific, emotional, and spiritual agreement here: repressed emotion contributes to real damage. Not just to your body, but to your relationships, your decisions, and your connection with God.

- Bitterness corrodes joy.
- Unprocessed grief hardens your heart.
- Suppressed fear turns into chronic stress.
- Shame turns into a mask you wear, even in worship.

Religious Environments Often Reward Suppression

Church culture doesn't always make space for emotion.

We reward the ones who keep it together. We elevate the polished. We celebrate quick turnarounds and miracle moments—but rarely do we disciple people through the process of emotional healing.

So what happens? People fake strength. They serve while broken. They preach while grieving. They lead while numb. They teach others how to be free while secretly drowning in suppressed pain.

Eventually, that internal tension shows up. In burnout. In moral failure. In breakdowns that no one saw coming. But it was coming all along. The soul just couldn't carry the weight anymore.

Common Ways We Suppress Emotion

1. Spiritualizing Everything
Sounds like: *"I don't need to feel, I just need more faith."*
Truth: Faith includes honest lament and emotional processing (read the Psalms!)

2. Avoidance or Numbness
Sounds like: *"I'm fine."* While avoiding conversations, journaling, or being still before God
Truth: If you avoid stillness, it's usually because something painful surfaces there.

3. Cynicism or Humor
Sounds like: *"It is what it is."* Joking away the pain.
Truth: Laughter isn't always healing if it hides a wound.

4. Over-Serving or Overworking

Sounds like: *"I don't have time to feel—I just need to keep going."*
Truth: Busyness is often a socially acceptable form of emotional escape.

Jesus Doesn't Shame You for Feeling

He is the High Priest who sympathizes with your weaknesses (Hebrews 4:15). He feels what you feel. He welcomes your honesty. He invites your sorrow. He doesn't need you to protect His image by pretending to be okay.

He already knows what's in you—and He's not afraid of it. He doesn't want your performance. He wants your presence.

Psalm 34:18 NIV — *"The Lord is close to the brokenhearted and saves those who are crushed in spirit."*

You don't need to clean up your feelings before coming to God. You bring your raw, real, messy heart—and He meets you there.

The Freedom in Lament

One of the lost disciplines of the modern church is lament—the spiritual practice of expressing sorrow, grief, and confusion before God. It's not complaining. It's not faithlessness. It's honesty. It's intimacy. It's what David did in Psalm after Psalm. And it's something Jesus did when He cried,

"My God, My God, why have You forsaken Me?"

Lament is what allows the pain to breathe before it breaks you. It's what brings the wound into the presence of the Healer. It's how you stop bleeding emotionally and start receiving wholeness.

What Happens When You Begin to Feel Again

When you stop suppressing and start surrendering:

- Tears begin to flow (sometimes for the first time in years).
- The tightness in your chest begins to lift.
- Compassion returns to places that were hardened.
- Worship becomes real again.
- Clarity begins to rise from the fog.
- You no longer need to run. You just need to be.

This is not weakness. This is freedom.

How to Stop Suppressing and Start Releasing

1. Name the Emotion
"What am I really feeling right now?" (fear, sadness, disappointment, anger, shame…)

2. Invite Jesus Into It
Don't fix it first. Just welcome Him into the feeling. Ask: "Jesus, where are You with me in this?"

3. Express It Honestly
Pray it out loud. Write it in a journal. Cry. Worship through it. Go for a walk and talk with God like David did.

4. Receive Comfort

Ask the Holy Spirit to minister to your heart. Let His truth speak—not to shut down the emotion, but to bring healing to it.

5. Repeat the Process Often

Wholeness doesn't come through a one-time cry. It's a rhythm. It's soul care. It's walking with God daily—emotionally present, spiritually aligned.

Reflection Questions

1. What emotions have I been taught (intentionally or unintentionally) to suppress?

2. In what areas of my life do I feel emotionally shut down or numb?

3. What am I afraid will happen if I actually let myself feel?

4. What would it look like to begin practicing lament and emotional honesty with God this week?

FOUR

David's Model

EXPRESSING THE HEART TO GOD

I f anyone could be called emotionally healthy in the Bible, it was David. Not because he never struggled— but because he knew what to do with what he felt. David wasn't perfect. He wasn't always composed. He didn't always get it right. But he was honest. He knew how to cry, shout, grieve, repent, rejoice, and hope— all in the presence of God.

He wrote songs in caves. He wept openly in defeat. He danced wildly in worship. He questioned God in despair. He confessed his darkest sins. And through it all, he kept coming back. David shows us what it looks like to live with a fully engaged soul—a soul that feels, processes, and communes with God in every season. This is the model we must reclaim if we're going to stop suppressing and start living fully alive.

A Man After God's Own Heart

David is described in Scripture as "a man after God's

own heart" (1 Samuel 13:14; Acts 13:22). That phrase doesn't mean he was morally perfect. It means he had a heart that relentlessly pursued God—honestly, humbly, and emotionally.

The Psalms, most of which were written by David, are not sterile devotionals. They are the soul on paper—raw, messy, volatile, and beautiful. Let's look at how David expressed his heart to God:

- Fear — "When I am afraid, I put my trust in You" (Psalm 56:3 ESV)
- Anger — "Break the teeth in their mouths, O God!" (Psalm 58:6 NIV)
- Grief — "My tears have been my food day and night…" (Psalm 42:3 ESV)
- Joy — "In Your presence there is fullness of joy…" (Psalm 16:11 ESV)
- Repentance — "Create in me a clean heart, O God…" (Psalm 51:10 ESV)

David didn't filter his prayers. He didn't hide his emotions. He brought his entire self to God. And that's why his soul didn't rot in silence—it thrived in surrender.

Pouring Out Your Heart Is Not a Lack of Faith

Psalm 62:8 NIV says,

"Trust in Him at all times, you people; pour out your hearts to Him, for God is our refuge."

To pour out your heart means to express what's inside —fully, honestly, without reservation. It's not doubting

God's goodness; it's trusting Him enough to bring your pain. It's not a sign of weak faith—it's a sign of relational faith. Faith that believes God is safe enough to hold your mess. David shows us that being real with God is part of intimacy with God. God doesn't want a performance. He wants proximity.

David Didn't Vent About God — He Processed With God

There's a difference between complaining in rebellion and pouring out your soul in brokenness. David never ranted about God behind His back—he brought his confusion to God's face. And because of that, his emotions didn't pull him away from God—they drew him deeper into trust. Psalm 13 is a perfect example:

"How long, Lord? Will You forget me forever? How long will You hide Your face from me?" (vv. 1–2 NIV)

But by verse 5, he shifts:

"But I trust in Your unfailing love; my heart rejoices in Your salvation."

David starts in pain and ends in praise. Why? Because he processed it all in God's presence. The venting turned into victory. The sorrow turned into surrender. The soul realigned with truth through emotional honesty.

David Worshiped Through Emotion, Not Around It

One of the most powerful things about David's

TOM CORNELL

example is that he didn't wait to feel good before he
worshiped. He brought his real-time emotions into
worship.

- When he was afraid, he still declared trust.
- When he was overwhelmed, he still turned his
  eyes upward.
- When he sinned, he didn't wallow—he
  repented and reached for God's mercy.

David teaches us that we don't worship after we get
healed—we worship in the process of healing. That's what
keeps the soul from going numb or bitter. That's how you
invite the Healer into the places that hurt.

Honest Emotions Lead to Real Encounters

When you look at David's life, you don't just see
emotional transparency—you see constant encounter. God
met him in the wilderness. God spoke to him in caves. God
comforted him after failure. God honored him with legacy.
And much of that flowed from David's willingness to feel.
To be still. To worship in tears. To lean in when he felt low.
Emotional honesty is not a detour from intimacy—it's the
doorway.

Your Psalms May Not Be Written Yet

Many people never realize how powerful their personal
worship could be— because they've never felt safe enough
to bring their soul to God like David did. But what if your
deepest healing is hidden in the conversation you've been
too afraid to have with God?

What if your tears are the ink for the psalms He wants you to write in secret? What if the presence you long for is waiting on the honesty you've been avoiding? You don't have to sing someone else's song. You just have to bring your real self before God—and let Him meet you there.

The Gift of Being Fully Known

David was fully known—and he still had God's favor.
He was exposed—and still called chosen.
He was flawed—and still given the throne.

This is the power of bringing your whole heart to God: you discover that He's not scared of your darkness, your sadness, your rage, or your tears. He sees all of it. And He stays. He draws near. He speaks. He comforts. He restores.

Practical Ways to Express Emotion Like David

<u>1. Journal Your Psalms</u>
Write out what you feel without editing. Then write out your declarations of truth and trust. This rhythm mirrors the psalms.

<u>2. Worship With Authenticity</u>
Don't fake it. Sing songs that align with your current emotional place—or sit in silence and let tears speak louder than words.

<u>3. Pray Emotionally, Not Just Logically</u>
Let your voice match your heart. God isn't grading your theology—He's inviting your honesty.

<u>4. Use the Psalms as a Mirror</u>

Find a psalm that expresses what you can't yet say. Read it aloud. Let David's words give voice to your silence.

Reflection Questions

1. What emotions have I avoided bringing to God?

2. When was the last time I poured out my heart in prayer like David?

3. Do I believe God can handle my raw emotions?

4. What's one area of my life where I need to worship through emotion rather than wait to feel better?

FIVE

Emotions Are Messengers, Not Masters

We live in a world of emotional extremes. Some people are ruled by their emotions—every high and low dictating their thoughts, actions, and relationships. Others suppress and silence emotion entirely, viewing feelings as unreliable or even unspiritual. But in the Kingdom of God, there is a better way.

Emotions are not evil. They're not weakness. They're not a sign of immaturity. They are messengers—signals sent from the soul. And when we learn to listen to those signals through the lens of the Spirit, we begin to walk in greater self-awareness, healing, and intimacy with God. The problem isn't emotion. The problem is when we let emotion drive instead of inform.

God Created You to Feel

God made you in His image—and that includes your emotional capacity. Throughout Scripture, we see God express emotion:

- He rejoices (Zephaniah 3:17)
- He grieves (Genesis 6:6)
- He gets angry (Exodus 32:10)
- He loves with deep compassion (Isaiah 49:15)

Jesus, too, lived with a full emotional range:

- He wept (John 11:35)
- He felt compassion (Matthew 9:36)
- He got angry at injustice (Mark 3:5)
- He was troubled and overwhelmed (Matthew 26:38)

If God Himself feels, then your emotional design is not a flaw—it's a feature. It's part of what makes you able to connect, empathize, discern, and love.

The Purpose of Emotion

Emotions are indicators, not dictators. They serve a purpose, but they were never meant to take the lead. Think of emotions like a check-engine light on your car. They don't tell you everything, but they tell you something is going on under the hood. You wouldn't rip the dashboard out just because the light came on— and you shouldn't ignore or shame your emotions either.

Here's how emotions serve you when surrendered to God:

- Emotions reveal what you value.

Joy points to fulfillment. Sadness points to loss. Anger points to injustice.

- Emotions expose what you believe.

Fear may signal that you're trusting in self over God. Guilt might reflect a lie that you're not truly forgiven.

- Emotions invite God into your story.

When you feel deeply, it opens the door to connection and healing in a way that intellectual agreement never could.

Discerning Emotion in the Spirit

Emotion by itself isn't always accurate. You might feel fear in a safe place. Or peace in the middle of compromise. That's why your emotions must be discerned, not dismissed or obeyed blindly.

Discernment helps you ask:

- Where is this emotion coming from?
- What is this feeling telling me?
- Is this based in truth or trauma?
- What does God want to do with this emotion?

For example:

- Fear can either be a lie of the enemy—or a God-given warning.

Sadness might signal unresolved grief—or a call to compassion for others.

- Anger could point to unhealed wounds—or righteous indignation against injustice.

The key is to process your emotion in the presence of the Holy Spirit. Emotions are safest when surrendered. They're clearest when brought into God's light.

When Emotions Become Masters

God gave you emotions to serve you, but when they rule you, they distort your vision. Here's what happens when emotions go from messengers to masters:

- You start reacting instead of responding.
- You make permanent decisions from temporary feelings.
- You interpret God's silence as abandonment.
- You lose emotional self-control and call it passion or authenticity.
- You justify sin because "that's just how I feel."

Proverbs 25:28 NIV warns us:

"Like a city whose walls are broken through is a person who lacks self-control."

In Kingdom living, feelings are felt—but truth makes the final decision. Emotions are part of the conversation, but not the conclusion.

What Emotionally Healthy People Understand

Emotionally healthy believers are not emotionally absent or emotionally explosive. They live in rhythm with both emotion and truth. Here's what they know:

1. They allow themselves to feel. They don't ignore or numb their soul.

2. They name what they feel. They can say, "I feel sad," or "I feel afraid," without shame.

3. They ask God into the emotion. They process with the Holy Spirit, not in isolation.

4. They align emotion with truth. They acknowledge the feeling but let truth guide the next step.

5. They choose wholeness over impulse. They don't always feel peace—but they walk in it anyway.

This level of maturity doesn't come overnight. It's cultivated over time as you practice surrender instead of suppression and alignment instead of avoidance.

Don't Ignore the Messenger

One of the most important lessons I've learned in my healing journey is this: God will often use your emotions to lead you to what He wants to heal.

- That frustration that keeps rising? It may point to an area where you feel unseen or powerless.

- That persistent sadness? It may uncover a loss you've never properly grieved.

- That anxiety that won't go away? It might be telling you there's an inner child still carrying fear.

If you keep ignoring the messenger, you'll miss the mercy that's being offered. The longer you deny your emotions, the longer you delay your healing.

How to Respond When Emotion Surfaces

1. Pause and Breathe, Give yourself space to feel without judgment. Take 5 minutes to check in with your soul.

2. Ask the Holy Spirit, "What is this feeling saying?" Emotions are rarely random. There's often a root.

3. Bring it into prayer. Write it out, say it out loud, or cry it out before the Lord. Let God meet you there.

4. Speak truth over the emotion. Affirm God's Word and promises—not to silence the feeling, but to realign it.

5. Ask what your soul needs. Do you need rest? Comfort? A boundary? Forgiveness? Healing from a lie?

Your soul's needs are not an interruption to your spiritual life—they are the place where transformation begins.

Jesus Felt Deeply, But Was Led by the Spirit

Jesus was not emotionally detached. He cried. He groaned. He rejoiced. But He was never ruled by emotion. He walked in the Spirit—and the Spirit led Him with compassion, wisdom, and power. That's our model: Spirit-led emotional wholeness. We don't need to shut down what we feel. We need to surrender what we feel to the Spirit of Truth.

Reflection Questions

1. Do I view emotions as dangerous, weak, or unspiritual?

2. How have I responded to emotional pain in the past—numbing, avoiding, overreacting?

3. What might God be trying to show me through a current emotion I've been ignoring?

4. How can I create space this week to listen to my emotions and let the Holy Spirit lead me through them?

SIX

The Hidden Cost of a Silenced Soul

A silenced soul is a dangerous soul. When your emotions are consistently ignored, your pain pushed down, and your needs left unmet, it doesn't just disappear—it hides. And what hides in the soul doesn't heal. It festers. It grows. It leaks. And over time, it begins to cost you more than you realize.

Most people don't collapse overnight. They wear a brave face, lead a small group, run a business, even preach a sermon—and yet their soul is quietly disintegrating behind the scenes. Because suppressed emotion doesn't stay silent forever. It speaks in the body. It reveals itself in relationships. It manifests in habits. It wears masks until it doesn't have the strength to anymore.

This chapter is a wake-up call—not to fear what's buried in your soul, but to bring it into the light before it costs you everything.

The Soul Can't Be Silenced Without Consequences

Proverbs 14:30 ESV says,

"A tranquil heart gives life to the flesh, but envy makes the bones rot."

David wrote in Psalm 32:3–4 NIV,

"When I kept silent, my bones wasted away through my groaning all day long. For day and night Your hand was heavy on me; my strength was sapped as in the heat of summer."

These verses aren't just metaphorical—they reflect the very real connection between your soul and your physical body. Emotional suppression leads to soul exhaustion. And soul exhaustion always demands payment somewhere.

The 3 Primary Costs of a Silenced Soul

1. Emotional Cost — Numbness and Reactivity. When you silence pain, you don't just avoid the bad—you lose access to the good. You can't selectively numb emotion. When you suppress sadness, you also dull your capacity for joy.

- You may stop crying, but you also stop laughing freely.
- You stop dreaming, hoping, engaging fully with life.

Eventually, numbness breaks—and when it does, it often comes out as reactivity:

- Quick tempers.
- Passive-aggressive remarks.
- Meltdowns over small things.

These are not random—they're the soul's way of saying, "You've ignored me too long."

2. Relational Cost — Walls, Withdrawal, and Wounds
A silenced soul doesn't know how to connect deeply with others.

- It builds walls to protect from pain.
- It withdraws rather than risk rejection.
- It creates confusion—others sense something is off, but they can't name it.

Over time, relationships become shallow, distant, or codependent. You may show up physically but be absent emotionally. You stop trusting. You stop sharing. And intimacy suffers—not just in marriage or friendship, but even in your walk with God.

3. Physical and Mental Cost — Anxiety, Fatigue, and Sickness

The body remembers what the mind tries to forget. Scientific studies confirm what Scripture has long taught: chronic emotional suppression is linked to increased anxiety, weakened immune response, high blood pressure, digestive problems, insomnia, and even autoimmune issues. Add to that the mental toll:

- Persistent brain fog
- Difficulty concentrating
- Overwhelm
- Panic attacks

It's not that your body is failing. It's that your soul is

overloaded. And your system is waving a white flag, begging you to stop pretending everything's fine.

Suppression Looks Like Strength Until It Breaks

We often admire people who seem stoic under pressure. The unshakable ones. The "strong, silent types." But make no mistake—emotional suppression isn't strength. It's survival. And it will eventually shatter.

I've walked with leaders, fathers, mothers, and pastors who did everything "right" on the outside—prayed, served, gave—but were silently dying inside. When the collapse finally came, it wasn't because they didn't love God. It was because they never gave their soul permission to speak. Unfelt emotion becomes a ticking time bomb. Not because emotion is bad, but because buried pain demands attention.

The Lies That Keep Us Silent

The enemy loves to plant thoughts that keep you locked in suppression. Lies like:

- "If I start feeling this, I won't be able to stop."
- "I'm overreacting."
- "God doesn't care about feelings—He wants obedience."
- "Other people have it worse."
- "I just need to get over it."

Each lie reinforces the internal prison. Each lie keeps you disconnected from your humanity and your healing. But here's the truth:

- You won't drown in your emotion when Jesus is your anchor.
- God cares about what you feel, not just what you do.
- You are not too emotional—you are unfinished. And He's still healing you.

Unmet Needs Become Open Doors

We don't just suppress pain—we suppress need. And unmet needs, when ignored, become vulnerabilities the enemy exploits. If your soul is crying for:

- Connection — you may run to pornography, fantasy, or unhealthy relationships.
- Comfort — you may turn to alcohol, food, or endless entertainment.
- Significance — you may overwork, perform, or chase affirmation.
- Safety — you may control, isolate, or avoid.

These aren't just "bad behaviors." They are coping strategies rooted in unaddressed need. The solution isn't just deliverance from the behavior—it's healing for the soul that's been trying to survive.

When the Church Misses the Soul

Too often, we've discipled people's spirits while ignoring their souls. We tell them to pray more, serve more, believe harder. But we don't sit with them in grief. We don't help them name their pain. We quote Scripture at people who need someone to weep with them first.

As a result, we create believers who perform but don't feel. Who obey but don't process. Who smile in the foyer but crumble in silence. The Kingdom doesn't operate like that. In the Kingdom, healing is holistic. Jesus didn't just teach truth—He touched lepers, listened to women's stories, wept with friends, and fed hungry souls. He healed both the spirit and the soul—and so must we.

Your Soul Is Worth Healing

You don't have to keep living numb. You don't have to keep pretending to be okay. The cost of staying silent is far greater than the discomfort of facing your pain. Jesus is not asking you to fix yourself. He's asking you to stop hiding.

He's already paid the price for your wholeness. He already sees the weight you've been carrying. And He's ready to walk with you—not just out of sin, but out of soul silence.

Practical Steps to Begin Releasing the Pressure

1. Start with Honesty
Admit to yourself and to God: "I've been suppressing things I don't know how to feel."

2. Listen to Your Body
Where do you carry tension or heaviness? What physical cues might be pointing to soul pain?

3. Talk to Safe People
You don't need to heal in isolation. Vulnerability brings strength when shared wisely.

4. Invite Jesus to the Root

Ask: "Jesus, where did I first learn that it's not okay to feel this?"

5. Start Writing or Speaking Aloud Daily
Give your soul space to breathe through journaling or verbal processing with God.

Reflection Questions

1. Where in my life have I been silencing my soul?

2. What emotional, physical, or relational symptoms might be tied to suppressed pain?

3. What beliefs have I held about emotions that need to be challenged?

4. Am I ready to let Jesus speak to the places I've worked so hard to silence?

SEVEN

Guarding the Heart Without Hardening It

"Above all else, guard your heart, for everything you do flows from it." —Proverbs 4:23 NIV

There's a difference between a guarded heart and a hardened one. A guarded heart is discerning, discerning what should come in and what must be kept out. A hardened heart is closed—defensive, numb, and often isolated.

In our journey of healing and emotional wholeness, we must learn to live with a guarded heart that remains soft, open, and alive—instead of a hardened one that self protects out of fear or past pain. Because healing doesn't just require release—it requires ongoing protection. And that protection must come from wisdom and love, not bitterness and avoidance.

What Does It Mean to Guard Your Heart?

Proverbs 4:23 doesn't say to guard your emotions, your

past, or your image. It says to guard your heart—your inner life. Why? Because everything flows from it. Your thoughts. Your behaviors. Your ability to connect, to discern, to dream. If your heart gets contaminated—by bitterness, fear, shame, or deception—it won't just affect you. It will affect everyone connected to you. Guarding your heart means:

- Paying attention to what you're letting into your soul.
- Staying emotionally and spiritually alert.
- Keeping yourself from false peace and false intimacy.
- Choosing truth, integrity, and vulnerability—on purpose.

It's not about living suspiciously. It's about living intentionally.

The Difference Between Guarding and Hardening

Here's how you can tell the difference:

- Discerns who is safe//Distrusts everyone
- Sets boundaries with love//Builds walls out of fear
- Processes pain with God//Pretends pain doesn't exist
- Responds with grace and clarity//Reacts with defensiveness or silence
- Stays open to growth and connection//Pulls away to avoid being hurt
- Knows when to say yes and no//Says never again to everyone

You're not protecting your healing if you're also isolating from your calling.

Pain Can Make You Harden If You're Not Watchful

Many people harden not because they're rebellious, but because they're wounded.

- They trusted the wrong person.
- They were emotionally manipulated.
- They gave their heart and it was trampled.
- They tried to be vulnerable and were shamed for it.

So the soul makes a vow: "That will never happen again." And with that vow, a wall is built. The wall feels safe. It feels strong. But over time, it becomes a prison. It keeps pain out—but it also keeps love out. And it eventually keeps God out too.

"Today, if you hear His voice, do not harden your hearts…"
(Hebrews 3:15 NIV)

This verse reminds us that a hardened heart isn't just closed to people—it's closed to God's voice. And when you can't hear clearly, you stop healing. You stop hoping. You stop dreaming.

Guarding Means Being Watchful, Not Fearful

To guard your heart is not to live in suspicion or paranoia. It's to live like a watchman on the wall—eyes open, spirit discerning, heart anchored in truth.

- You watch for intrusive thoughts that don't belong.
- You check the motives behind decisions.
- You stay alert to spiritual atmospheres.
- You steward your emotional boundaries with wisdom.

Guarding your heart means asking:

- "What is shaping my emotions right now?"
- "What am I meditating on in this season?"
- "Am I protecting my peace or avoiding my pain?"
- "Am I creating boundaries or building barriers?"

Boundaries Are Kingdom. Walls Are Fear-Based.

Jesus Himself had boundaries. He walked away from crowds. He didn't entrust Himself to everyone. He chose intimacy with the few. He said "no" without apology. And He still lived open, powerful, and free.

Boundaries are a form of soul stewardship. They are not selfish—they are strategic. They tell the world, "This space matters. I am not my own—I belong to the Lord."

Walls, on the other hand, are built in panic, pain, and self-protection. And they often don't just keep people out—they lock you in. You were never called to build walls. You were called to build altars.

How to Guard Without Hardening

1. Stay Emotionally Honest Before God

When you notice yourself pulling away from people, opportunities, or even God —pause. Ask, "Is this wisdom… or fear?"

2. Let the Holy Spirit Be Your Filter

Every conversation, invitation, and connection should pass through Him. Ask, "Holy Spirit, is this for me?"

3. Be Quick to Forgive and Slow to Isolate

Forgiveness doesn't mean re-entering toxic environments. But it does mean releasing bitterness so your heart stays clean.

4. Practice Sabbath for the Soul

Regular rest, reflection, and solitude keep your heart soft. Stillness creates space for God to tend to what's beneath the surface.

5. Stay in Safe Relationships

Don't guard your heart by being alone. Guard it by choosing community that calls you higher, listens with compassion, and speaks the truth in love.

Your Heart Was Made to Be Alive

A truly guarded heart is one that is fully alive—feeling, discerning, loving, choosing, repenting, forgiving, rejoicing. It doesn't flinch at sorrow. It doesn't shut down under pressure.

It doesn't explode in chaos. It flows—with grace, clarity, joy, and power. That's what Jesus is after in you. Not just a healed heart. A whole heart. A guarded heart. A free heart.

What Are You Guarding It For?

You guard something because it's valuable.

God is not asking you to harden your heart. He's asking you to guard it like treasure. Because it is. It's the wellspring of your life. It's the place where His Spirit dwells. It's the launching point of your purpose. And if you lose your heart, you'll lose the clarity and strength to fulfill your call.

A guarded heart is not a closed heart. A guarded heart is a clean heart—anchored, open, and protected by love.

Reflection Questions

1. Where in my life have I built walls instead of setting healthy boundaries?

2. Am I guarding my heart from lies and toxicity—or from love and truth?

3. What relationships or situations may require clearer boundaries?

4. How can I invite God to help me protect my peace while keeping my heart soft?

EIGHT

When Trauma Hijacks Your Emotions

N ot all pain is the same. Some wounds you feel and recover from quickly. Others leave a deeper mark.

Trauma is what happens when pain overwhelms your soul's ability to process or protect itself. It's not just what happened to you—it's what happened in you as a result. It leaves a fingerprint on the nervous system, a script in your thoughts, and often a silence in your voice. And most importantly—it shapes how you feel, how you react, and how you relate.

You can be saved, gifted, called—and still be emotionally hijacked by unhealed trauma.

What Is Trauma?

Trauma is more than a painful event. It's the unresolved impact of that event on the soul and nervous system. Trauma says:

- "It's not safe to trust."
- "I have to take care of myself."
- "Feelings are dangerous."
- "I'm always going to be left."
- "I can't let anyone in."

It often causes the soul to:

- Disconnect from emotions.
- Freeze in fear when triggered.
- React aggressively or retreat quickly.
- Interpret love as danger.
- Live in constant alert, even in peace.

The effect is that you begin to live through a lens shaped by survival, not wholeness. Even in safe places, you still scan for threats. Even in loving relationships, you brace for rejection. You don't live—you defend.

Types of Trauma

1. Acute Trauma
A single event—abuse, accident, loss, betrayal— that overwhelms your ability to cope.

2. Chronic Trauma
Ongoing exposure to fear, chaos, neglect, manipulation, or emotional abandonment.

3. Developmental Trauma
Wounds formed during formative years—often due to inconsistent caregiving, absence of comfort, or emotional misattunement.

4. Spiritual Trauma

Pain caused by abuse of spiritual authority, toxic church environments, manipulation using Scripture, or abandonment in your time of need.

You don't have to compare your trauma to someone else's. If it hurt you deeply and changed the way you feel, think, or relate—it matters.

The Soul's Survival Response

When trauma hits, your brain and body move into survival mode—fight, flight, freeze, or fawn.

- Fight — You become aggressive, defensive, reactive.
- Flight — You avoid, run, distract, or become hyper-busy.
- Freeze — You shut down, go numb, dissociate, or feel stuck.
- Fawn — You appease, people-please, or lose your voice to stay safe.

These are not just personality quirks. They're trauma responses. They were once necessary to survive. But when they go unhealed, they shape a life that never truly rests.

Trauma Distorts Emotion

Unhealed trauma trains your emotions to respond not to the present moment, but to a past wound. You may be in a healthy marriage but still feel abandoned when your spouse is quiet. You may be serving in a loving church but still feel unsafe every time someone corrects you.

You're not crazy. You're not rebellious. You're reacting to a history that hasn't been healed. Here's how trauma distorts emotional response:

- You overreact in moments that don't require it.
- You under-feel in moments that should move you.
- You become hyper-vigilant—always scanning for danger.
- You feel powerless to stop certain feelings or behaviors.
- You feel ashamed for reacting but don't know how to change.

Until trauma is healed, it keeps interrupting your emotions, hijacking your peace, and shaping your relationships.

Jesus Doesn't Just Heal the Surface—He Heals the Root

Jesus came to "bind up the brokenhearted" (Isaiah 61:1 NKJV). This means He doesn't just forgive your sins or cleanse your past—He heals the shattered places in your soul. He's not afraid of your flashbacks, your shutdowns, your grief.

He doesn't shame you for how you react—He lovingly walks you back to where the pain began and restores you there. Where religion says, "Just move on," Jesus says, "Let's go back and heal that together."

The Healing Journey: From Reaction to Restoration

You may not be able to erase the event. But with Jesus, you can heal the impact. You can unhook the trauma from your nervous system. You can rewire the way you feel, react, and respond. Here's how the healing journey unfolds:

1. Recognize the Pattern
Notice recurring reactions, triggers, or emotional spirals that don't match the current moment.

2. Name the Root
Ask the Holy Spirit: "Where did I first feel this way?"
Memories may surface—not to retraumatize, but to redeem.

3. Invite Jesus Into the Pain
Picture Him with you in the memory. Let Him speak, comfort, defend, restore. He was there even when you didn't know it.

4. Release the Emotions
Let the tears come. Let the shaking happen. Let your body process what it had to store. Your soul is safe in His hands.

5. Receive His Truth and Peace
Ask: "Jesus, what do You say about me in this place?" Let His truth replace the lie that trauma taught you.

6. Renew Your Reactions
Begin to live from healing, not from hypervigilance.

Set new patterns. Practice pause, peace, and presence.

Healing Doesn't Mean Forgetting—It Means Freedom

Healing from trauma doesn't mean the memory disappears. It means the sting is gone. The power is broken. The emotions don't hijack you anymore. You're not afraid of your past—you've been restored in it. And because of that, you can now:

- Respond with grace instead of fear
- Stay grounded in love instead of retreating in shame
- Be present in joy without bracing for pain

You Are Not Broken. You Are Becoming Whole.

Trauma tried to write your story, but Jesus is the Author now. You are not too far gone. You are not stuck forever. You are not damaged goods.

You are a son. A daughter. A temple of the Spirit. And Jesus is walking with you—not just toward destiny, but into deep emotional wholeness. This is what freedom really feels like—not numb, not reactive, but alive.

Reflection Questions

1. Are there emotional reactions in my life that feel disproportionate or hard to control?

2. What traumatic memories or seasons might still be shaping how I feel and respond?

3. Have I invited Jesus into those painful memories—or have I tried to avoid them?

4. What would it look like for my emotional life to be rooted in peace instead of protection?

NINE

Healing the Suppressed Heart

HOW TO RELEASE PAIN TO GOD

S ome wounds are loud—sharp, obvious, explosive. Others are quiet—deep, lingering, buried beneath layers of survival. But all unprocessed pain eventually demands a voice. And if you don't give it one through surrender, it will find one through dysfunction.

Suppressed pain doesn't just sit still. It becomes anxiety, bitterness, addiction, depression, perfectionism, overcommitment, or emotional withdrawal. And while we may learn to manage the symptoms, true healing only happens when we bring the pain to God and release it—fully, honestly, and with expectation of His comfort and restoration.

This chapter is your invitation to stop carrying what Jesus is ready to heal.

Pain Was Never Meant to Be Carried Alone

Jesus never expected you to carry your trauma, your betrayal, or your grief by yourself. He never told you to stuff it, power through it, or pretend it didn't hurt. The invitation has always been:

"Come to Me, all who are weary and burdened, and I will give you rest." —Matthew 11:28 NIV

Pain becomes toxic when it's hoarded in the soul instead of handed over to the Healer.

But many believers don't release pain because they've never been shown how. They're told to let go—but never taught what that actually means. So they live stuck between knowledge and breakthrough. Free in name but bound in emotion.

What Does It Mean to "Release" Pain to God?

To release pain doesn't mean to ignore it, spiritualize it, or shove it aside. It means to bring it into full view—to feel it, speak it, and surrender it in God's presence. It's not catharsis for the sake of venting. It's honesty that leads to healing.

It looks like:

- Crying before God instead of numbing.
- Speaking truthfully in prayer instead of reciting safe phrases.
- Letting tears, silence, or shaking happen without shutting it down.
- Opening the locked room of your heart and saying, "Jesus, come into this too." You're not just dumping pain—you're giving it to the only One strong enough to carry it and loving enough to redeem it.

The Suppressed Heart: Signs and Symptoms

You may be suppressing pain if you often:

- Feel disconnected from your own emotions
- Experience frequent tightness in the chest or shallow breathing
- Struggle with sudden emotional overreactions
- Have a short fuse but deep internal pressure
- Default to "I'm fine" when asked how you're doing
- Avoid silence, solitude, or journaling
- Can't cry, even when you want to
- Struggle to remember details from painful seasons

Suppression is not strength. It's the soul's survival instinct when it hasn't been given space to heal. But what protected you in the past may be preventing you from freedom now.

The Process: How to Release Pain to God

Here's a practical framework for walking through the healing process of releasing emotional pain to God. Take your time. Go slow. Let the Spirit lead.

1. Pause and Acknowledge the Pain

Start by slowing down. Breathe deeply. Ask yourself: What am I really feeling? You might identify:

- Grief
- Disappointment

- Betrayal
- Anger
- Fear
- Shame
- Loneliness

Name the feeling. Bring it into the light. It loses power the moment it's acknowledged in truth.

2. Trace the Pain to Its Root

Where did this start? When have I felt this before?

Let the Holy Spirit bring up a memory, a moment, or a pattern. It may be something recent, or something buried from years ago. Don't panic—He's not bringing it up to shame you. He's showing you where He wants to heal.

3. Invite Jesus Into the Memory

This is the moment everything changes.

Close your eyes and picture that painful place. The room. The moment. The emotion. Then ask: "Jesus, where were You?" Let Him show you how He was present, even when it didn't feel like it. Let Him speak truth into the lie. Let Him comfort the part of you that froze in that moment. Let Him rewrite the narrative.

4. Express the Pain Fully

Let your body and voice participate. Cry. Speak. Journal. Sit in silence. Worship.

Don't censor your feelings. Don't rush the moment. Let the pressure release. This is not weakness—it's divine exchange. You are giving Jesus what you were never meant to carry.

5. Forgive, If Needed

Unforgiveness often locks pain in place. Ask Jesus to help you forgive anyone involved in your pain—family, friends, leaders, yourself.

Say aloud: *"I choose to forgive ____ for ____. I release them into Your hands."*

Forgiveness doesn't say what they did was okay. It says, "I refuse to carry the consequences of their sin anymore."

6. Break Agreement with the Lie

Every wound tries to teach a lie.

- "I'm unlovable."
- "I'm always alone."
- "God doesn't protect me."
- "My voice doesn't matter."

Speak aloud: *"I break agreement with the lie that ____. I come into agreement with the truth that ____."*

Declare truth over your heart. Use Scripture. Declare who God is. Remind your soul what's real.

7. Ask Jesus for His Gift in Exchange

Ask Him: "Jesus, what do You want to give me in place of this pain?"

Sometimes it's a word. Sometimes a picture. Sometimes peace floods in where sorrow once lived. Let Him finish the healing moment by sealing it with His presence and joy.

8. Rest and Receive

You may feel tired. Spent. That's okay. Your soul has just released a burden it's carried for too long. Breathe. Rest. Let the healing settle.

Why This Matters

This process may feel foreign. Maybe no one ever told you it was okay to feel. Maybe you've been taught to "be strong," "move on," or "get over it." But this is what Jesus came to do: "to bind up the brokenhearted."

This is how your soul breathes again.
This is how the pressure lifts.
This is how joy returns—not as hype, but as healing.
You don't get free by ignoring the pain.
You get free by walking through it with Jesus.

Practical Prompts for Releasing Pain

Try these during your next prayer time:

- "Jesus, what pain am I carrying right now that You want to take?"

- "Holy Spirit, show me the first place I felt this emotion."
- "Father, what lie did I believe in that moment?"
- "What truth do You want me to know instead?"
- "What do You want to give me in exchange for what I'm releasing?" Let the answers come gently. Don't force it. Trust the Spirit to lead.

Reflection Questions

1. What emotions or memories have I suppressed that God may be inviting me to release?

2. What lie have I been believing about myself, God, or others because of this pain?

3. What would change in my life if I fully released this to God?

4. Am I ready to feel again—not to fall apart, but to finally heal?

TEN

Rebuilding Emotional Integrity

LIVING FROM A WHOLE HEART

Healing is not just about what you let go of—it's about what you begin to walk in. After you release pain, break agreements, and surrender suppressed emotions to Jesus, there comes a new invitation: to rebuild. To live from a whole heart, not a fractured one. To walk in emotional integrity—where what you feel, believe, and express are aligned with truth, love, and spiritual maturity.

Emotional integrity is not perfection. It's consistency. It's the ability to walk honestly with God, yourself, and others without hiding, performing, or fragmenting who you are. And it's the fruit of healing—not just a healed event, but a healed identity.

What Is Emotional Integrity?

Emotional integrity is the harmony between:

- What you feel
- What you believe

- How you respond

It means you don't have to fake joy, pretend you're okay, or explode under pressure. It means your emotional life is anchored, not erratic. You know when you're sad and let yourself process. You feel anger but don't sin. You notice fear but choose trust. You experience emotion but live under truth.

This kind of living is rare—but it's possible when your heart has been healed and aligned by the Spirit of God.

A Whole Heart Isn't a Perfect Heart — It's a Connected One

Psalm 86:11 NIV says: "Give me an undivided heart, that I may fear Your name."

A whole heart isn't one without weakness—it's one that's no longer divided by fear, shame, pretense, or unhealed pain. It's a heart connected to God and integrated in its parts. It doesn't split off into masks or personas. It doesn't compartmentalize. It doesn't live in survival mode. It lives in truth, presence, and purpose.

When you're emotionally whole:

- Your feelings become indicators, not drivers.
- Your needs are acknowledged and brought to God instead of suppressed.
- Your relationships are built on authenticity instead of performance.
- Your emotional life is surrendered, not silenced.

Five Traits of Emotionally Whole People

1. They Feel Freely but Don't Live in Reaction

They allow space for sadness, joy, anger, and grief—but they don't let emotions hijack their values or decisions. "Be angry, and do not sin…" (Ephesians 4:26 NKJV) They feel deeply. But they respond wisely.

2. They Align Emotion with Truth

They don't invalidate their feelings—but they don't idolize them either. They submit what they feel to what is true and allow God's Word to realign their perspective.

3. They Know What They Need

Emotionally healthy people can identify their needs—comfort, connection, rest, encouragement—and seek them in life-giving, Spirit-led ways. They don't ignore their soul or medicate their needs with sin.

4. They Cultivate Safe and Honest Relationships

They are vulnerable without oversharing, open without being emotionally dependent. They invite others into their process but take responsibility for their growth. They speak the truth in love and receive correction without collapse.

5. They Worship from Wholeness, Not Hiding

Their worship is not just emotional—it's embodied, anchored in their full self. They bring their joy, their sorrow, and their questions into God's presence. They don't perform for God—they commune with Him.

Wholeness Requires Rhythm, Not Just Revelation

Healing moments are powerful. But wholeness is built in daily rhythm. It's not just one altar call or one emotional breakthrough. It's what you do next. You stay whole by:

- Checking in with your soul daily
- Processing with God before reacting toward others
- Journaling or praying through emotions weekly
- Creating space for joy, rest, laughter, and reflection
- Staying rooted in truth and committed to community

Wholeness is not a destination. It's a lifestyle of soul stewardship.

The Role of the Holy Spirit in Emotional Integrity

The Holy Spirit isn't just your Helper in ministry— He's your Comforter in healing. He teaches you how to live emotionally integrated.

- He reminds you of truth when your feelings lie.
- He calms your nervous system with His presence.
- He gives you the gift of discernment—helping you separate real emotions from false conclusions.
- He helps you pause, breathe, and respond rather than react.
- He brings supernatural peace in places where anxiety once ruled.

You don't need emotional strength as much as you need emotional surrender. The Spirit fills surrendered space.

Walking in Wholeness Doesn't Mean You Won't Be Triggered

Even after healing, you'll still face situations that tempt your soul to revert to old patterns. But wholeness doesn't mean never being triggered. It means knowing what to do when you are.

When you feel the rise of anger, the temptation to shut down, the fear of rejection —you stop. You breathe. You ask the Holy Spirit, "What's happening in my soul?"

And you respond with truth instead of trauma. That's emotional maturity.

Wholeness Makes You a Safe Place for Others

Emotionally healthy people become safe places— homes for others' vulnerability, not judges of it. When you are emotionally whole:

- You stop projecting your pain on others.
- You start listening instead of fixing.
- You create space for others to be honest.
- You disciple with compassion, not control.

The Church doesn't need more perfect leaders. It needs more whole ones. People who are emotionally honest, Spirit-led, and unafraid to bring both wounds and worship to Jesus.

Your Wholeness Is Part of Your Witness

In a culture full of anxiety, volatility, and emotional instability, your healed heart becomes a testimony. Your joy has weight. Your peace carries power. Your calm in chaos shines like light in darkness.

People won't just ask what you believe—they'll ask how you live with that kind of inner stability. And the answer will be: "Because Jesus didn't just save me—He made me whole."

Reflection Questions

1. Where in my life do I still react emotionally instead of responding with truth?

2. What new habits can I build to stay emotionally whole?

3. Am I living connected—between what I feel, believe, and do—or is there fragmentation?

4. How can I grow in emotional maturity without losing emotional authenticity?

ELEVEN

Soul Care as a Lifestyle

Your soul doesn't just need rescue—it needs rhythm. We often treat soul healing like a crisis intervention. A breakdown happens. Emotions boil over. Trauma resurfaces. So we run to a conference, call for prayer, or finally have that hard conversation. And while God absolutely meets us in those powerful breakthrough moments, true transformation is sustained through daily choices, not just emotional encounters.

Soul care is not a trend. It's a Kingdom discipline. It's not self-indulgence—it's stewardship. When your soul is healthy, your spirit flourishes, your mind is clear, your emotions are manageable, and your relationships are richer. But when your soul is neglected, everything else eventually begins to break down.

If you want to walk in lasting wholeness, you need more than healing. You need habit.

Jesus Lived in Rhythms of Soul Care

Jesus was fully God and fully man, but He didn't neglect His humanity. He intentionally stepped away from crowds. He regularly withdrew for solitude. He rested. He wept. He had long meals with friends. He honored the Sabbath. He processed His emotions in prayer.

"But Jesus often withdrew to lonely places and prayed." —Luke 5:16 NIV

Jesus didn't just minister from power—He ministered from wholeness. And He guarded it by keeping a rhythm that nourished His soul. If Jesus needed space to breathe, reflect, process, and be alone with the Father, how much more do we?

The Goal of Soul Care Is Connection, Not Control

Soul care isn't about fixing yourself. It's not another religious task list. The goal is to stay connected—to God, to your inner world, to truth, and to life-giving people.

- It's not about mastering emotion—it's about noticing it.
- Not about avoiding pain—it's about walking with Jesus through it.
- Not about managing behavior—it's about cultivating awareness and intimacy.

Soul care isn't about perfection—it's about rhythm. It's the daily practice of showing up for your inner life with compassion and surrender.

Six Soul-Care Rhythms for Daily Wholeness

1. Stillness and Silence

The soul thrives in stillness. Even 10–15 minutes of silence each day can help you become aware of what you're carrying.

- Start your day in quiet—no phone, no noise.
- Sit before God and ask: "What's going on in my heart today?"
- Let silence reveal what words can't.

"Be still and know that I am God." (Psalm 46:10 NIV)

2. Journaling and Reflective Prayer

- Writing helps your heart speak.
- Journal your emotions, thoughts, and prayers.
- Track triggers, patterns, and breakthroughs.
- Let God respond to your writing in His Word and whispers.

This is how you begin to know your soul—and let the Spirit tend to it.

3. Sabbath and Rest

Sabbath isn't optional for the soul. It's oxygen.

- Designate one day a week for rest, joy, worship, and reset.
- Say no to productivity. Say yes to presence.
- Let your soul exhale.

"The Sabbath was made for man, not man for the Sabbath…"
(Mark 2:27 NIV)

4. Emotion Check-Ins with the Holy Spirit

Pause throughout the day and ask:

- "What am I feeling?"
- "Why am I feeling it?"
- "What do I need to bring to God right now?"

Don't wait until you're overwhelmed. Process in real-time.

5. Authentic Relationships

You don't heal in isolation. You need safe, Spirit-filled community.

- Build relationships where you can be honest and challenged.
- Let others speak truth, hold you accountable, and remind you who you are.
- Practice being emotionally present, not just physically present.

6. Daily Re-Alignment with Truth

Feelings are real, but they're not always reliable. Align daily.

- Read and declare Scripture that speaks to your identity and freedom.

- Use truth to re-center your emotions—not suppress them, but anchor them.

Signs Your Soul Needs Attention

- You're numb emotionally or overwhelmed constantly.
- You snap easily, even at small things.
- You feel spiritually dry but don't know why.
- You're busy but disconnected from joy.
- You feel exhausted even when you rest.
- You haven't cried, laughed, or worshiped deeply in a long time.
- You're reactive rather than responsive.

These aren't just life symptoms—they're soul signals. Pay attention. Don't shame yourself—tend to yourself.

Common Myths That Keep People from Soul Care

Myth 1: "I don't have time."
Truth: You don't have time not to. Everything flows from your soul. A few minutes daily will save hours of emotional fallout later.

Myth 2: "This is selfish."
Truth: Self-neglect is not godly. Jesus said to love others as you love yourself (Mark 12:31 NIV). You can't give what you don't have.

Myth 3: "If I slow down, I'll fall apart."
Truth: Slowing down is where Jesus meets you. He holds what you're afraid to feel. Healing is not a breakdown—it's a breakthrough.

Soul Care Is a Weapon Against the Enemy

When your soul is neglected, the enemy has more room to operate:

- Lies feel louder.
- Temptation feels stronger.
- Discouragement feels heavier.
- Discernment gets clouded.
- Identity feels unstable.

But when your soul is cared for, you become a fortress. You can stand in the storm. You can lead others with peace. You can hear God clearly. You can resist the enemy with confidence. Your inner life is not a luxury—it's a battleground. Guard it.

Make It Sustainable, Not Superficial

You don't need an hour-long soul care routine. You need a rhythm that fits your real life:

- 10 minutes of silence before work.
- A weekly walk with worship music.
- Five-minute emotion check-ins.
- One honest conversation each week.
- Bedtime journaling.
- A monthly personal retreat.

Simple. Sustainable. Transformational.

God Cares About the Pace of Your Soul

He's not impressed with your busyness. He's not asking

you to sprint. He wants to walk with you in the cool of the day again—just like in Eden.

He cares about your rest.

He cares about your laughter.

He cares about your pace.

He cares about your internal world.

Let Him slow you down. Let Him restore your rhythm. Let Him bring you back to yourself—the "you" He designed to live, not just survive.

Reflection Questions

1. Which soul-care rhythm do I most need to implement right now?

2. What lie have I believed about rest, reflection, or emotional maintenance?

3. What's one simple change I can make this week to care for my soul more intentionally?

4. How might my relationships, spiritual life, and leadership change if I truly lived from a cared-for soul?

TWELVE

A Safe Place for Others

CREATING A CULTURE OF EMOTIONAL WHOLENESS

Wholeness is never just about you. Everything God does in your soul—every tear, every truth, every healing moment—is meant to overflow into someone else's life. You are not just a healing project. You are a healing conduit. And when emotional integrity becomes your lifestyle, your very presence begins to carry healing.

People feel safer around healed people.

They don't always know why. They just know they can breathe. They feel seen. They stop pretending. They sense they won't be judged, rushed, or dismissed. Something in your story gives them permission to be honest in theirs. And that's exactly what Jesus did—He created safe space for the soul to exhale.

Jesus Was the Safest Person on Earth

Jesus was emotionally whole. That's why people came to Him in their worst moments —crying, bleeding, grieving, exposed. Not because He was soft, but because He was safe. His holiness didn't repel them—it drew them in.

- The woman with the issue of blood risked public shame just to touch Him.
- Zacchaeus, a hated tax collector, came down from the tree and repented without force.
- Peter wept bitterly after denying Jesus yet he knew Jesus would take him back.

Jesus didn't minimize pain. He didn't rush repentance. He didn't skip over people's stories. He made room for them—and they walked away transformed. Your wholeness makes you a safe place like that too.

Healing People Help Heal People

You don't have to be fully arrived to be used.

You just have to be honest, humble, and present.

When your soul has encountered God's healing, you begin to carry:

- Compassion over criticism
- Patience over pressure
- Empathy over embarrassment
- Curiosity over control

You stop demanding perfection. You start walking with people where they really are. You disciple differently. You listen more. You lead with love. And others begin to feel safe enough to stop hiding.

How to Become a Safe Place for Others

1. Be Authenti `cally You

Healed people don't wear masks. They don't perform. They live connected to who they are in Christ, even when they're still in process.

- Share your story with vulnerability, not shame.
- Don't hide your current struggles—model how to walk through them with God.
- People are drawn to real, not impressive.

2. Practice Deep Listening

Sometimes the most healing thing you can do is listen without fixing. Let people feel. Let them talk longer than is comfortable. Let them cry without filling the silence.

- Don't offer advice too quickly.
- Don't hijack their pain with your story.
- Ask Spirit-led questions like, "Where do you think God is in this?" or "What do you need from Him right now?"

3. Hold Space Without Control

A safe leader doesn't force, manipulate, or demand. They create an atmosphere of peace and clarity where God does the heavy lifting.

- You don't need to be everyone's solution. Be a door to His solution.
- You don't need to rush people's process. Be present while God works.
- You don't need to have all the answers. Your posture of love is often enough.

4. Honor Boundaries and Emotions

Safe people respect emotional process without pushing or dismissing it.

- "That sounds really painful. I'm here to walk with you."
- "I can see how that would make you feel unheard. Let's ask God what He wants to say about that."
- "Would you like to pray, process, or just sit together?" Honor creates a container where healing can happen.

Creating a Culture of Emotional Wholeness in Ministry and Family

You can't disciple people deeply if their souls don't feel safe around you. Whether you lead a family, a team, a church, or a friend group—emotional safety is the soil where growth happens. Here's how to cultivate it:

Normalize Emotion

Let it be okay to talk about feelings without shame. Model it. Preach it. Live it.

- "What are you feeling right now?" is a great discipleship question.
- Don't just ask, "What did God say?" Also ask, "How did that make you feel?"

Lead with Testimony, Not Pressure

Instead of forcing people into vulnerability, lead with yours. It opens the door for others.

- Share what Jesus healed in you.
- Talk about your process, not just your breakthrough.
- Let people know it's okay to be in the middle.

Create Safe Environments for Honest Process

Make space in your small groups, prayer meetings, or even staff culture for honesty.

- Start meetings with a soul check-in.
- Give room for prayer and processing, not just strategy.
- Protect confidentiality and foster honor.

What Emotional Wholeness Creates in Community

When a culture of emotional integrity grows, here's what begins to emerge:

- People repent more freely because they're not afraid of being shamed.
- Conflict is handled in love, not avoidance or explosion.
- Discipleship goes deeper, because the soul is engaged, not just behavior.
- Marriages are restored, because both hearts feel safe enough to be seen.
- Worship becomes authentic, because people are no longer hiding.
- Children grow up emotionally aware and spiritually grounded, because their parents didn't raise them in silence.

This is Kingdom culture—not just power, but presence. Not just miracles, but maturity of heart.

Wholeness Becomes Reproducible

What God does in you becomes the blueprint for others. Your healing becomes a model. Your rhythms become contagious. Your story becomes a doorway.

You stop striving to be impressive. You start becoming impactful. You stop trying to "help" people. You start hosting a space where God does what only He can.

That's what emotionally whole people do. They carry healing. They reproduce it. They multiply it.

You Are a Living Invitation

Your life can say:

- "You don't have to hide anymore."
- "You can bring your full self to God."
- "You can cry and still be strong."
- "You can heal, even from that."
- "You can be whole—and you don't have to do it alone."

This is your legacy. This is your calling. Not to be the Savior—but to be a safe place where the Savior meets broken hearts and makes them whole.

Reflection Questions

1. Do people feel safe enough to be emotionally honest around me?

2. How can I cultivate deeper emotional integrity in my family, church, or team?

3. What might change in my relationships if I slowed down and listened better?

4. Who in my life needs a safe place to process—and how can I offer it?

Conclusion

WHOLE, HEALED, AND FULLY ALIVE

You were never meant to live half-alive. You weren't created to numb your emotions just to keep functioning, to carry silent pain just to keep performing, or to bury your soul just to protect your calling. That's not strength. That's survival. And it's time to stop surviving and start living.

Wholeness is your inheritance. Not perfection. Not performance. Not emotional denial. Wholeness. Deep, Spirit-led, heart-connected, emotionally honest wholeness.

It's what Jesus died for. It's what the Holy Spirit is forming in you. And it's what the world is starving to see— a generation of believers whose outer lives are not built on the fractured foundation of suppressed inner worlds, but on healed hearts, renewed minds, and restored souls.

This Is the Invitation

This book was never just a manual for self-help. It's been an invitation from the Father. An invitation to:

- Come out of hiding
- Reclaim the voice of your soul
- Stop calling suppression strength
- Bring your tears into His presence
- Rebuild your inner world around truth
- And carry emotional wholeness as a Kingdom witness in a broken world You're not weak for needing this. You're wise for responding.

The Fruit of Wholeness

A whole soul doesn't mean an unshakable life.

It means when the shaking comes, you don't break. You bend. You process. You grieve. You listen. You adjust. You pray. You let others in. You keep walking.

From this place of wholeness, you'll begin to see:

- Your relationships deepen with honesty and grace
- Your ministry flows from compassion, not compulsion
- Your peace remains even when your circumstances shift
- Your joy returns, no longer based on control but on connection
- Your identity stabilizes, rooted in God's truth, not people's opinions

This is what it means to be whole, healed, and fully alive.

You Are a Signpost for Others

The way you live from now on is not just
about you.
Your emotional integrity will shape your children.
Your surrendered heart will create room for
someone else's healing.
Your peace will become a refuge.
Your honesty will break cycles.
Your tears will water new growth in those who are
still afraid to feel.
You are not just walking out of brokenness.
You're walking others out too.

It's Not Too Late

You may have lived decades with numbness. You may
have ignored the tightness in your chest, the avoidance in
your habits, the shortness in your tone. You may have even
led others while quietly bleeding inside. But the mercy of
God is this: as long as you're breathing, your soul can heal.

Today can be a new rhythm. A new response. A new
awareness. You don't need a title, a platform, or a counseling
degree. You just need a heart that says: "Jesus, I want to live
whole. I give You my emotions. I give You my thoughts. I
give You my pain. And I trust You to walk me into peace."

What Comes Next

The journey doesn't end here. This is a beginning.

- Keep tending to your soul with the Spirit daily.

- Keep naming emotions and aligning them with truth.
- Keep breaking lies and building new declarations.
- Keep sitting in stillness. Keep journaling your heart.
- Keep being a safe place for others to process.
- Keep inviting Jesus into everything.

And when you slip—and you will—don't shame yourself. You're not back at the start. You're still on the path. Grace carries you forward. This isn't about living pain-free. It's about living present.

This isn't about being emotionless. It's about being emotionally anchored. This isn't about never feeling again. It's about feeling with Jesus next to you.

The Final Word: Jesus, Our Wholeness

At the center of all this is not a process—it's a Person. Jesus is the Shepherd of your soul.

He doesn't just restore your behavior—He restores you.

He walks with you through the valley. He defends you against the accuser. He speaks truth into your silence. He invites you to weep, to rejoice, to feel, and to follow.

He is not in a hurry with your healing.

He is not frustrated by your emotions.

He is not distant when you break down.

He is near. And He's making you whole—day by day, layer by layer, glory to glory.

So keep walking. Keep opening. Keep surrendering.

Because you were made to be whole, healed, and fully alive.

Let it be so, Lord.

Make us a people who live from healed souls— vessels of peace in a world of noise, safe places in a world of judgment, honest disciples in a world of masks.

Let Your Church be whole again.

Let our souls come alive again.

In Jesus' name. Amen.

30-Day Soul Wholeness Activation Guide

Daily Rhythms to Cultivate Healing, Awareness, and Spirit-Led Emotional Integrity Each day includes:

- A Scripture
- A Reflection Prompt
- A Prayer Activation

WEEK 1: Awakening the Soul

Day 1
Scripture: Psalm 139:23–24
Prompt: What am I feeling today—mentally, emotionally, physically?
Prayer: Search me, God. Reveal anything in my soul that needs healing or attention.

Day 2
Scripture: 2 Corinthians 10:5
Prompt: What thoughts have I agreed with that don't align with God's Word?

Prayer: I take every thought captive. Expose the lies I've believed and replace them with truth.

Day 3
Scripture: Psalm 62:8
Prompt: When was the last time I truly poured out my heart to God?
Prayer: God, I come to You raw and honest. Here is what I'm carrying…

Day 4
Scripture: Proverbs 14:30
Prompt: Where has suppressed pain shown up in my body, mood, or relationships?
Prayer: Heal my soul, Lord, and let that healing flow into my physical and emotional health.

Day 5
Scripture: John 11:35
Prompt: What pain am I afraid to feel?
Prayer: Jesus, You wept. Teach me how to weep with You and not be ashamed of emotion.

Day 6
Scripture: Psalm 42:11
Prompt: What emotion keeps surfacing again and again lately?
Prayer: I invite You into this feeling, Lord. Help me hear what my soul is trying to say.

Day 7
Scripture: Matthew 11:28
Prompt: What burdens have I been trying to carry alone?

Prayer: Jesus, I lay down the pressure I've placed on myself. Give me rest.

WEEK 2: Releasing the Pain

Day 8
Scripture: Psalm 32:3–5
Prompt: What memory do I avoid because it still carries pain?
Prayer: I invite You into that memory, Jesus. Show me where You were and what You say now.

Day 9
Scripture: Isaiah 61:1–3
Prompt: Where in my life do I still feel broken-hearted?
Prayer: Bind up my heart, Lord. Trade my ashes for beauty and my mourning for joy.

Day 10
Scripture: John 14:26–27
Prompt: What would peace feel like in my body and mind today?
Prayer: Holy Spirit, teach me the way of peace. Settle my soul in Your presence.

Day 11
Scripture: Romans 12:2
Prompt: What lie have I believed about myself or my value?
Prayer: I break agreement with the lie that ___. I receive the truth that ___.

Day 12

Scripture: 1 Peter 5:7
Prompt: What anxiety or emotional pressure do I need to cast on Jesus?
Prayer: I cast this on You, Jesus. I trust You to hold me steady.

Day 13

Scripture: Psalm 147:3
Prompt: Where has my soul been fragmented or numb?
Prayer: Heal my fractured parts, Lord. Make me whole again.

Day 14

Scripture: Philippians 4:6–7
Prompt: What is stealing my sense of peace right now?
Prayer: With thanksgiving, I bring this to You. Guard my heart and mind in Christ.

WEEK 3: Rebuilding Identity and Emotional Strength

Day 15

Scripture: Galatians 4:7
Prompt: Do I see myself as a son/daughter or as an orphan trying to survive?
Prayer: Remind me who I am. I am Yours. I belong to a family.

Day 16

Scripture: Romans 8:1
Prompt: Where have I been condemning myself or carrying guilt?

Prayer: There is no condemnation in Christ. I receive Your mercy today.

Day 17
Scripture: Isaiah 43:19
Prompt: What new thing is God trying to do in my heart?
Prayer: I let go of the old. Do a new work in me, even in my emotions.

Day 18
Scripture: 2 Timothy 1:7
Prompt: Where do I still feel powerless or fearful?
Prayer: I receive power, love, and a sound mind. I am not a slave to fear.

Day 19
Scripture: Proverbs 4:23
Prompt: What do I need to guard in my heart today?
Prayer: Help me protect my peace without hardening my heart.

Day 20
Scripture: Psalm 23:3
Prompt: Where do I need restoration and rest in my soul?
Prayer: Shepherd of my soul, restore me. Lead me beside still waters again.

Day 21
Scripture: Psalm 51:10
Prompt: What needs to be cleansed from my emotional life—jealousy, resentment, pride?

Prayer: Create in me a clean heart, O God, and renew a steadfast spirit within me.

WEEK 4: Living Whole and Becoming a Safe Place

Day 22
Scripture: Hebrews 4:15–16
Prompt: Am I approaching God boldly, or still hiding parts of myself?
Prayer: I draw near today—fully seen, fully loved. Thank You for Your grace.

Day 23
Scripture: James 1:19–20
Prompt: Am I quick to listen and slow to react emotionally?
Prayer: Teach me to respond from wholeness, not wounds.

Day 24
Scripture: Colossians 3:12–14
Prompt: How am I reflecting emotional maturity in my closest relationships?
Prayer: Clothe me in compassion, kindness, humility, gentleness, and patience.

Day 25
Scripture: 1 Thessalonians 5:23–24
Prompt: What area of my life still needs sanctification—spirit, soul, or body?
Prayer: Sanctify me completely, Lord. Finish what You started in me.

Day 26

Scripture: John 15:5

Prompt: Am I abiding or striving today?

Prayer: Apart from You, I can do nothing. Keep me rooted in You.

Day 27

Scripture: Matthew 5:9

Prompt: Am I a peacemaker in my home, church, or team?

Prayer: Let me carry peace, not just keep peace. Heal others through my presence.

Day 28

Scripture: Romans 15:13

Prompt: What hope do I need to rekindle in my heart?

Prayer: Fill me with all joy and peace as I trust in You, so I may overflow with hope.

Day 29

Scripture: Psalm 73:26

Prompt: Where am I weak today—and what does God want to strengthen?

Prayer: Though my heart may fail, You are the strength of my heart forever.

Day 30

Scripture: Isaiah 61:3

Prompt: What has God done in my soul these last 30 days?

Prayer: Thank You, Lord, for turning my mourning into dancing, my ashes into beauty.

I receive the oil of joy and the garment of praise. I am whole. I am Yours.

About the Author

Tom Cornell is the Senior Leader of SOZO Church in Washington state, founder of Walk in the Light International and SOZO Network. Tom is married to his beautiful wife Katy and lives in the Puget Sound area with her and their three kids. He has been in ministry pastoring and teaching the body of Christ since 2008.

He has a passion to see the body of Christ moving from people with an orphan mindset to that of sonship; equipping the body to do the work of Jesus resulting in seeing the Kingdom of God manifested here on earth.